Professional Driver Reveals Rapid Credit Repair System

If you need help go to my website:

UrbanCreditSecrets.com or email me at
UrbanCreditRepairSolutions@gmail.com   Jason Kirkwood

Content

Professional Driver Reveals Rapid Credit Repair System

LET'S GET STARTED

The Main Axis Players

Yes they are the axis and you should treat them like they are the enemy.

There are 4 players on the axis side

Experian Equifax TransUnion

Fico

FICO (NYSE: FICO) is a software company based in San Jose, California and founded by Bill Fair and Earl Isaac in 1956. Its FICO score, a measure of consumer credit risk, has become a fixture of consumer lending in the United States.

Thing to know

1) There are 3 different credit bureaus. TransUnion, Equifax and Experian.

2) All of these companies have different reports on you. This is because they don't share information on you with each other. They are competitors with each other. Each wants their own information, it's how they make money.

3) These CRA's (credit reporting agencies **are not affiliated with the government**. They are private companies.

4) They make money by selling your information to businesses who want to see if you are credit worthy. Think of it like you own a furniture shop. You want to make more sales and extend credit. You don't know the customers personally. You are willing to pay $5 to find out if this customer pays other merchants back.

5) They use FICO to determine a score for each person. They pay FICO (Fair Isaac and Company) for their mathematical formula.

Where do the Credit Reporting Agencies Get there information

In the U.S., consumer reporting agencies collect and aggregate personal information, financial data, and alternative data on individuals from a variety of sources called data furnishers with which the reporting agencies have a relationship.

Data furnishers are typically creditors, lenders, utilities, debt collection agencies (credit bureaus) and the courts (i.e. public records) that a consumer has had a relationship or experience with. Data furnishers report their payment experience with the consumer to the credit reporting agencies.

The data provided by the furnishers as well as collected by the bureaus are then aggregated into the consumer reporting agency's data repository or files. The resulting information is made available on request to customers of the consumer reporting agencies' for the purposes of credit risk assessment, credit scoring or for other purposes such as employment consideration or leasing an apartment.

Given the large number of consumer borrowers, these credit scores tend to be mechanistic. To simplify the analytical process for their customers, the different consumer reporting agencies can apply a mathematical algorithm to provide a score the customer can use to more rapidly assess the likelihood that an individual will repay a particular debt given the frequency that other individuals in similar situations have defaulted.

What's on Your Credit Report

Although each credit reporting agency formats and reports this information differently, all credit reports contain basically the same categories of information.

Your social security number, date of birth and employment information are used to identify you. These factors are not used in credit scoring. Updates to this information come from information you supply to lenders.

Identifying Information.

Professional Driver Reveals Rapid Credit Repair System

Your name, address, Social Security number, date of birth and employment information are used to identify you. These factors are not used in credit scoring. Updates to this information come from information you supply to lenders.

Trade Lines.

These are your credit accounts. Lenders report on each account you have established with them. They report the type of account (bankcard, auto loan, mortgage, etc), the date you opened the account, your credit limit or loan amount, the account balance and your payment history.

Credit Inquiries.

When you apply for a loan, you authorize your lender to ask for a copy of your credit report. This is how inquiries appear on your credit report. The inquiries section contains a list of everyone who accessed your credit report within the last two years.

The report you see lists both "voluntary" inquiries, spurred by your own requests for credit, and "involuntary" inquires, such as when lenders order your report so as to make you a pre-approved credit offer in the mail.

Public Record and Collections.

Credit reporting agencies also collect public record information from state and county courts, and information on overdue debt from collection agencies. Public record information includes bankruptcies, foreclosures, suits, wage attachments, liens and judgments.

What's Not on Your Credit Report

Prepaid Debit Cards, Checking Accounts, and Traditional Debit Cards

None of these aforementioned items appear on your credit reports. Debit cards and checking accounts are really the same thing, as a debit card is like a plastic version of a paper check.

And, a prepaid debit card is really not much more than a reloadable gift card with fees.

None of the three items are a true extension of credit, as you're only able to spend money that is already either: A) loaded on the card, or B) deposited in an account with a bank or credit union.

Professional Driver Reveals Rapid Credit Repair System

If you need help go to my website:

UrbanCreditSecrets.com or email me at
UrbanCreditRepairSolutions@gmail.com   Jason Kirkwood

There is considerable confusion over the prepaid debit card and credit reporting issue because some of the companies and individuals who are paid to endorse these cards suggest they will help your credit reports and scores, which isn't at all true.

In fact, the credit bureaus now have language in their reporting standards guide that addresses the issue of prepaid debit cards and credit reporting.

It reads, "Do not report prepaid credit cards/gift cards because the consumer has no credit obligation."

There is, however, one scenario when your checking account could bleed into your credit report: If you have overdraft protection in the form of an unused installment loan that loan can be reported to the credit bureaus.

I personally have one of these on my credit reports and have had it for many years.

Evidence That You Are Now Married
When you get married nobody in the credit industry knows about it.

The credit reporting agencies don't know about it, your credit scores don't know about it, and lenders don't know about it.

There is nothing on a credit report that appears or changes just because you've gotten married.

Now, if you choose to apply jointly with your new spouse or you otherwise co-mingle your existing debt obligations and liabilities, then eventually your credit reports will look similar to your spouse's credit reports because the data will be so similar.

Want some great advice?

Maintain credit independence even after you're married.

There's no reason to co-mingle your debts and there's no reason to jointly apply for credit, except in the instance where you'll need two incomes to qualify for a loan.

Wealth Metrics

There's nothing on a credit reports that indicates your salary, your net worth, your debt-to-income ratio, or the amount of money in your wallet, 401K, IRA, SEP, Money Market, brokerage account, or any other savings account.

There is no way to presume someone's income by looking at his or her credit reports.

This shouldn't be a surprise because credit reports are supposed to tell a story about your creditworthiness, not your income.

Income and other wealth metrics are measurements of capacity, or your ability to pay a bill. Credit reports and credit scores are supposed to tell a story about whether or you'll choose to pay your bills.

Public Utilities and Medical Bills
While there are exceptions to this rule most of the time your public utilities and medical bills do not appear on your credit reports month after month like a credit card or auto loan obligation.

If you do see a public utilities or medical bills on a credit report, they are likely there because they've gone into default and are being "worked" by a collection agency.

When a utility or medical bill goes into default, the service provider will normally outsource the collection of that bill to a debt collector.

And, debt collectors commonly report liabilities to the credit reporting agencies.

How is your Credit Score (FICO) calculated

The credit score, commonly referred to as a FICO score, is a proprietary tool created by the Fair Isaac Corporation. This is not the only way to get a credit score, but the FICO score is the measure that is most commonly used by lenders to determine the risk involved in a particular loan.

Due to the proprietary nature of the FICO score, the Fair Isaac company does not reveal the exact formula it uses to compute this number. However, what is known is that the calculation is broken into five major categories with varying levels of importance. These categories, with weight in brackets, are payment history (35%), amount owed (30%), length of credit history (15%), new credit (10%) and type of credit used (10%).

All of these categories are taken into account in your overall score - no one area or incident determines your score.

The payment history category reviews how well you have met your prior obligations on various account types.

It also looks for previous problems in your payment history such as bankruptcy, collections and delinquency. It takes into consideration the size of these problems, the time it took to resolve them, and how long it has been since the problems appeared. The more problems you have in your credit history, the weaker your credit score will be.

The next largest component is the amount that you currently owe to lenders. While this category focuses on your current amount of debt, it also looks at the number of different accounts and the specific types of accounts that you hold. This area is focused on your present financial situation, and a large amount of debt from many sources will have an adverse effect on your score.

The other categories (length of credit history, new credit and type of credit used) are fairly straightforward.

The longer you have a good credit history, the better. Common sense dictates that someone who has never been late with payment over twenty years is a much safer bet than someone who has been on time for two.

Also, people who apply for credit a lot probably already have financial pressures causing them to do so, so each time you apply for credit, your score gets dinged a little. And finally, a person with only one credit card is less risky than a person with 10, so the more types of credit accounts you have, the lower your score will be.

Professional Driver Reveals Rapid Credit Repair System

It is important to understand that your credit score only looks at the information contained on your credit report and does not reflect additional information that your lender may consider in its appraisal. For example, your credit report does not include such things as current income and length of employment.

Category	Description	Weight[5]
Payment history	how timely and consistent your payments are	40%
Depth of credit	length of credit history and types of credit previously received	21%
Utilization	debt-to-credit ratios and how much credit is available	20%
Balances	what your total debt is, most likely; delinquent debt is counted more harshly than current debt	11%
Recent credit	how recent and many new hard inquiries and new accounts there are	5%
Available credit	how much credit can be accessed, for example, could you spend $50,000 of credit tonight or within the next week	3%

Credit Score Ranges

There are several types of FICO credit score: classic or generic, bankcard, personal finance, mortgage, installment loan, auto loan, and NextGen score.

The generic or classic FICO score is between 300 and 850, and 37% of people had between 750 and 850 in 2013. According to FICO, the median classic FICO score in 2006 was 723, and 711 in 2011. The U.S. median classic FICO score 8 was 713 in 2014.

The FICO bankcard score and FICO auto score are between 250 and 900. The FICO mortgage score is between 300 and 850. Higher

scores indicate lower credit risk.

Each individual actually has more than 49 credit scores for the FICO scoring model because each of three national credit bureaus, Equifax, Experian and TransUnion, has its own database.

Data about an individual consumer can vary from bureau to bureau. FICO scores have different names at each of the different credit reporting agencies: Equifax (BEACON), TransUnion (FICO Risk Score, Classic) and Experian (Experian/FICO Risk Model). There are four active generations of FICO scores:

1998 (FICO 98), 2004 (FICO 04), 2008 (FICO 8), and 2015 (FICO 9 Consumers can buy their classic FICO Score 8 for Equifax, TransUnion, and Experian from the FICO website (myFICO), and they will get some free FICO scores in that moment (FICO Mortgage Score 2 (2004), FICO Auto Score 8, FICO Auto Score 2 (2004), FICO Bankcard Score 8, and FICO Bankcard 2 (2004). Consumers also can buy their classic FICO score for Equifax (version of 2004; named Score Power) in the website of this credit bureau, and their classic FICO Score 8 for Experian on its website.

NextGen Risk Score

The NextGen Score is a scoring model designed by the FICO company for assessing consumer credit risk. This score was introduced in 2001, and in 2003 the second generation of NextGen was released. In 2004, FICO research showed a 4.4% increase in the number of accounts above cutoff while simultaneously showing a decrease in the number of bad, charge-off and Bankrupt accounts when compared to FICO traditional. FICO NextGen score is between 150 and 950.

Each of the major credit agencies markets this score generated with their data differently:

Experian: FICO Advanced Risk Score
Equifax: Pinnacle
TransUnion: FICO Risk Score NextGen (formerly Precision)

Prior to the introduction of NextGen, their FICO scores were marketed

Professional Driver Reveals Rapid Credit Repair System

under different names:

    Experian: FICO Risk Model
    Equifax: BEACON
TransUnion: FICO Risk Score, Classic (formerly EMPIRICA)

VantageScore

VantageScore is the name of a credit rating product that was created by the three major credit bureaus (Equifax, Experian, and TransUnion). The product was unveiled by the three bureaus on 14 March 2006. The VantageScore is an attempt to compete with the FICO score produced by FICO.

VantageScore vs FICO

VantageScore and FICO score are different credit scores. FICO and the credit bureaus have allowed the public to know some information about the credit score categories and the corresponding calculation weights. FICO allows consumers get their generic or classic FICO score for Experian, TransUnion, and Equifax from myFICO website.

Consumers can get their VantageScores from free credit report websites for a fee, and TransUnion and Experian offer their VantageScore to consumers through their websites. All three agencies use the same formula to calculate the VantageScore; however, there are still discrepancies between the resulting scores if run for each of the credit reports.

This is due to different data the three agencies have on the credit reports. FICO, the original creator of the FICO Score, was not involved with the creation of VantageScore's new formula.

The three agencies have advertised the VantageScore as something that will help banks and lenders further drill down into the "subprime" categories. Subprime lenders are banks or other lenders dedicated to borrowers with less than perfect credit or harder to substantiate credit

The old VantageScore goes from 501 to 990, as reported by TransUnion:

    A: 900–990
    B: 800–899

C: 700–799
D: 600–699
F: 501–599

The VantageScore 3.0, the newest version, is between 300-850 from 2013.

While the exact details of how the score is calculated are unknown, VantageScore has released the categories and proportions used.

What contributes to a positive score in each category, and to what degree particular data affect the score, is unknown.

The score is meant to indicate the likelihood that a customer will pay the loan back on time and in a consistent manner; values which show behavior contrary to these are more likely to worsen the score, and vice versa.

YOUR ALLIES

What is the "Fair Credit Reporting Act"

The Fair Credit Reporting Act, 15 U.S.C. § 1681 ("FCRA") is U.S. Federal Government legislation enacted to promote the accuracy, fairness, and privacy of consumer information contained in the files of consumer reporting agencies.

It was intended to protect consumers from the willful and/or negligent inclusion of inaccurate information in their credit reports. To that end, the FCRA regulates the collection, dissemination, and use of consumer information, including consumer credit information.

Together with the Fair Debt Collection Practices Act ("FDCPA"), the FCRA forms the foundation of consumer rights law in the United States.

It was originally passed in 1970, and is enforced by the US Federal Trade Commission, the Consumer Financial Protection Bureau and private litigants.

The Fair Credit Reporting Act, as originally enacted, was title VI of Pub.L. 91–508, 84 Stat. 1114, enacted October 26, 1970, entitled An Act to

Professional Driver Reveals Rapid Credit Repair System

amend the Federal Deposit Insurance Act to require insured banks to maintain certain records, to require that certain transactions in United States currency be reported to the Department of the Treasury, and for other purposes.

It was written as an amendment to add a title VI to the Consumer Credit Protection Act, Pub.L. 90–321, 82 Stat. 146, enacted June 29, 1968.

Consumer Reports

Commonly referred to as credit reports, a consumer report "contains information about your credit - and some bill repayment history - and the status of your credit accounts.

This information includes how often you make your payments on time, how much credit you have, how much credit you have available, how much credit you are using, and whether a debt or bill collector is collecting on money you owe. Credit reports also can contain rental repayment information if you are a property renter.

It also can contain public records such as liens, judgments, and bankruptcies that provide insight into your financial status and obligations.

The FCRA Regulates

The FCRA regulates:

Consumer reporting agencies;
Users of consumer reports; and,
Furnishers of consumer information.
If a consumer's rights under the FCRA are violated, they can recover:

Actual or statutory damages;
Attorney's fees;
Court costs; and,
Punitive damages if the violation was willful. "The threat of punitive damages under 1681n of the FCRA is the primary factor deterring erroneous reporting by the reporting industry."

Professional Driver Reveals Rapid Credit Repair System

If you need help go to my website:

UrbanCreditSecrets.com or email me at
UrbanCreditRepairSolutions@gmail.com   Jason Kirkwood

Furnishers of Information

A creditor, as defined by the FCRA, is a company that furnishes information to consumer reporting agencies. Typically, these are creditors, with which a consumer has some sort of credit agreement (such as credit card companies, auto finance companies and mortgage banking institutions).

Other examples of information furnishers are collection agencies (third-party collectors), state or municipal courts reporting a judgment of some kind, past and present employers and bonders. Lenders have an important role to play in ensuring credit reports are accurate. Under the FCRA, creditors who furnish information about consumers to consumer reporting agencies must:

Provide complete and accurate information to the credit reporting agencies;
Investigate consumer disputes received from credit reporting agencies;
Correct, delete, or verify information within 30 days of receipt of a dispute; and,
Inform consumers about negative information which is in the process of or has already been placed on a consumer's credit report within one month.
(This notice doesn't have to be sent as a separate notice, but may be placed on a consumer's monthly statement. If sent as part as the monthly statement, it needs to be conspicuous, but need not be in bold type. Required wording (developed by the US Federal Treasury Department):

Notice before negative information is reported: We may report information about your account to credit bureaus. Late payments, missed payments, or other defaults on your account may be reflected in your credit report.

Notice after negative information is reported: We have told a credit bureau about a late payment, missed payment or other default on your account. This information may be reflected in your credit report.

Professional Driver Reveals Rapid Credit Repair System

Consumer Reporting Agencies

Consumer reporting agencies (CRAs) are entities that collect and disseminate information about consumers to be used for credit evaluation and certain other purposes, including employment. Credit bureaus, a type of consumer reporting agency, hold a consumer's credit report in their databases. CRAs have a number of responsibilities under FCRA, including the following:

CRAs must maintain reasonable procedures to ensure the maximum possible accuracy of the information contained within a consumer's report;
Provide a consumer with information about him or her in the agency's files and take steps to verify the accuracy of information disputed by a consumer;
If negative information is removed as a result of a consumer's dispute, it may not be reinserted without notifying the consumer in writing within five days; and,
Remove negative information seven years after the date of first delinquency (except for bankruptcies (10 years) and tax liens (seven years from the time they are paid).

The three big CRAs—Experian, TransUnion, and Equifax—do not interact with information furnishers directly as a result of consumer disputes. They use a system called **E-Oscar.**
In some areas of the country, however, there are other credit bureaus.

Nationwide Specialty Consumer Reporting Agencies

In addition to the three big CRAs, the FCRA also classifies dozens of other information technology companies as "nationwide specialty consumer reporting agencies" that produce individual consumer reports used to make credit determinations. Under Section 603 of the Fair Credit Reporting Act, the term "nationwide specialty consumer reporting agency" means a consumer reporting agency that compiles and maintains files on consumers on a nationwide basis relating to:

Medical records or payments;

Residential or tenant history;
Check writing history;
Criminal background; and,
Other public record information.

Because these nationwide specialty consumer reporting agencies sell consumer credit report files, they are required to provide annual disclosures of their report files to any consumer who requests disclosure. A partial list of companies classified as nationwide specialty consumer reporting agencies under FCRA includes: Telecheck, ChoicePoint, Acxiom, Integrated Screening Partners, Innovis, the Insurance Services Office, Tenant Data Services, LexisNexis, Retail Equation, Central Credit, Teletrack, the MIB Group, United Health Group (Ingenix Division), and Milliman.

Although the major CRAs Experian, Equifax, and TransUnion are required by law to provide a central source website for consumers to request their reports, the nationwide specialty consumer reporting agencies are not required to provide a centralized online source for disclosure. The FCRA Section 612 merely requires nationwide specialty consumer reporting agencies to establish a streamlined process for consumers to request consumer reports, which shall include, at a minimum, the establishment by each such agency of a toll-free telephone number for such consumer disclosure requests.

What the CRA's Should Do

This is what Credit Bureaus should do when they receive a Dispute Letter.

An employee at the Credit Bureau receives the dispute and personally reviews it. During this review they gather information and documents in regards to the disputed account by contacting the original creditor or collection agency (Data Furnisher).

The Credit Bureau Employee then reviews copies of original documents like the Credit Application, Billing Statements, Billing and Payment Statements or notes in the account looking for any errors in reporting. If anything is in question they will request proof from the "Data

Professional Driver Reveals Rapid Credit Repair System

Furnisher."

Once a full investigation has been completed, the Credit Bureau Employee will then update the consumer's account according to the results of the investigation.

This is great and Santa will bring your presents this year. This never happens.

Here's What Really Happens With Disputes

Credit bureaus use "Optical Character Recognition" or OCR which is part of their e-OSCAR system. This technology allows them to scan the consumer's letters and convert them into plain text that can be stored into a database. This way, they can deal with the over 20,000 dispute letters that they receive each day.

Your Credit Has Been Outsourced

Thanks to this technology and overseas outsourcing, credit bureaus have reduced that cost of each dispute from around $4.50 down to around 90 cents.

When the letter is received by the Credit Reporting Agency (Credit Bureau) it's electronically scanned with "Optical Character Recognition" and Matched against a DATABASE or "Boiler Plate" of Dispute Letters commonly used by Credit Repair Companies or found in cheap software programs and Credit Repair Books. If the algorithms find that your letter "matches" one of these letters in their database, your dispute will most likely be flagged as Frivolous, suspicious or it is simply ignored.

If you use poor or simplistic Credit Repair Software or Dispute Letters out of Credit Repair Books you might have firsthand experience with this.

No matter who writes the dispute letters or how threatening they are, if the scanned version DOES NOT match that of a "Boiler Plate" dispute letter used thousands of times, the scanned version will then be sent electronically overseas for processing. There, an outsource employee will look at the scanned dispute and assign a 3 digit code (even if it has Multiple pages of detailed documentation supporting the claim). Around

85% of disputes will fall under the same 5 codes.

E-Oscar Explained

e-OSCAR is a web-based, Metro 2 compliant, automated system that enables Data Furnishers (Credit Issuers like Bank of America Visa Credit Card and Collection Agencies like NCO Financial), and Credit Reporting Agencies (CRAs) to create and respond to consumer credit history disputes (the Dispute Letters that you mail to them).

Credit Reporting Agencies (CRAs) include Equifax, Experian, Innovis and TransUnion, their affiliates or Independent Credit Bureaus and Mortgage Reporting Companies. e-OSCAR also provides for Data Furnishers (DFs) to send "out-of-cycle" credit history updates to Credit Reporting Agencies (Equifax, Experian, Innovis and TransUnion).

The system primarily supports Automated Credit Dispute Verification (ACDV) and Automated Universal Data form (AUD) processing as well as a number of related processes that handle registration, subscriber code management and reporting. This system was created to reduce the overhead caused by about 20 thousand dispute letters received by the CRAs every day.

Thru the e-OSCAR system, the dispute processor reads the dispute and classifies it under a dispute code selected from a menu. Of these dispute codes, 85% of disputes fall under the same 5 codes. As you can see in the following chart, more than 50% of the disputes are grouped under the classifications of "Not mine and Account Status" which seem to be the more common mistakes incurred by Credit Reporting Agencies.

E-Oscar Codes

001 Not his/hers.
002 Belongs to another individual with same/similar name.
006 Not aware of collection.
008 Late due to change of address & never received statement.
010 Settlement or partial payments accepted.
012 Claims paid the original creditor before collection status or paid before charge-off.
014 Claims paid before collection status.

Professional Driver Reveals Rapid Credit Repair System

019 Included in the bankruptcy of another person.
023 Claims account closed.
024 Claims account closed by consumer.
031 Contract cancelled or rescinded.
037 Account included in bankruptcy.
038 Claims active military duty.
039 Insurance claim delayed.
040 Account involved in litigation.
041 Claims victim of natural or declared disaster.
100 Claims account deferred.
101 Not liable for account (i.e., ex-spouse, business).
102 Account reaffirmed or not included in bankruptcy.
103 Claims true identity fraud/account fraudulently opened.
104 Claims account take-over, fraudulent charges made on account.
105 Disputes Dates of Last Payment/Opened/of First Delinquency/Billing/Closed.
106 Disputes present/previous Account Status/Payment History Profile/ Payment Rating.
107 Disputes Special Comment/Compliance Condition Code/narrative remarks.
108 Disputes Account Type or Terms Duration/Terms Frequency or Portfolio Type disputed.
109 Disputes current balance.
110 Claims company will change.
111 Claims company will delete.
112 Claims inaccurate information.

Thru the e-OSCAR system, the dispute processor reads the dispute and classifies it under a dispute code selected from a menu. Of these dispute codes, 85% of disputes fall under the same 5 codes. As you can see in the following chart, more than 50% of the disputes are grouped under the classifications of "Not mine and Account Status" which seem to be the more common mistakes incurred by Credit Reporting Agencies.

Reasons of Dispute Percentages

Reason of Dispute	% of Disputes
Not Mine	31%
Account Status	21%
Inaccurate Information	17%
Account Amounts	9%
Account Closed	7%
Disputes Fall Under Same 5 Codes:	**85%**

Once your dispute is converted to one of the "Standardized Dispute Codes" within the e-OSCAR system, the code is sent via e-OSCAR to the Data Furnisher (the Original Creditor or Collection Agency) using a standardized form known as an Automated Credit Dispute Verification Form (ACDV).

When the data furnisher receives an ACDV thru the e-OSCAR system they should begin an "in-depth" investigation. If the furnisher is a Collection Agency, they should contact the Original Creditor for real documentation on the account, but the data furnisher will never receive nor see all the documentation part of the dispute.

Data Furnishers can receive thousands of disputes a month. e-OSCAR's solution to the problem is to send the Data Furnisher all these disputes in one large file (batch file), all at one time. When the data furnisher receives this file, there are several options for processing the data. One such option is called reply all.

This option allows the data furnisher to select a response like "Account Verified" and apply this response to multiple records in the file with a single click.

Another function called "Auto-Populate" allows the data furnisher to Auto Populate responses of ACDV before submitting them back to the credit bureau via the e-OSCAR system.

Attacking the Axis

Get Your Spies (Credit Monitoring)

Remember this is a war.

You can get a copy of all three reports here for free but

DON'T GET YOUR REPORTS HERE

www.annualcreditreport.com

18

Professional Driver Reveals Rapid Credit Repair System

If you use this site credit bureaus have 45 instead of 30 days to respond.

You need this time line to your advantage.

NEVER USE ANNUALCREDITREPORT.COM

So AGAIN NEVER USE THIS SITE

www.annualcreditreport.com

What is Credit Monitoring

Credit monitoring is a service that acts like a watchdog over your credit file and notifies you of any major changes to it so you are quickly alerted to any fraud on your accounts. Because the activities of fraudsters opening accounts in your name will show up first on your credit report within 30 days, especially when they fail to make payments on fraudulent accounts in your name, credit monitoring is helpful in detecting fraud on your accounts. The problem with credit monitoring is that it only catches the thievery once your accounts have already been hacked or used fraudulently and so it cannot protect your accounts from fraud or hacking.

Keeping tabs on your credit accounts can also show you your progress when trying to repair or build your credit, so credit monitoring is also very helpful in knowing where your credit stands

You need to monitor your credit so you can see your progress with credit repair.

Now remember you have 3 FICO Scores

Monitoring TransUnion and Equifax

Here are the two spy's you need. Now you will be able to monitor what all three of your scores are doing in real time. This is an absolute must.

You can access your Trans Union and Equifax. FICO score for free on

www.CreditKarma.com.

They use the Calculation using the Vantage Score 3.0 model, these scores range from 300 to 850.
Why Use CreditKarma.com

Monitoring Experian

You can access your Experian report and score here.
http://www.experian.com/
Introductory price of $4.95 for your first month of access, then just $19.95 each additional month. Cancel anytime if not satisfied.

Credit score calculated based on FICO® Score 8 model.

Score 8, are designed to predict the ... versions range from 250-900 (compared to 300-850 for base FICO® Scores

Keep this service until your credit is cleaned up.

SPY'S CAN BE TRAITORS

All three major credit bureaus have arbitration agreements in their terms of use,

That means if you buy your credit report online and find an error on it, you can still dispute the error. However, if you disagree with how the credit bureau managed the dispute and want to take the bureau to court, the credit bureau can legally press the arbitration clause and force you to give up your right to argue your case before a jury.

That can make it much more difficult to prove your case and win substantial damages if you've been financially wronged, say consumer lawyers.

In arbitration, your complaint will be handled by an individual arbitrator, appointed from an arbitration association chosen by the credit bureau, and it will be solely up to the arbitrator to decide your case. If you disagree with the arbitrator's decision, you are not allowed to appeal.

Forced arbitration clauses never help the consumer.

Professional Driver Reveals Rapid Credit Repair System

They only help the business that does something wrong.

You NEED TO mail an opt-out letter to the credit bureau's within 30 to 60 days of receiving the report.

TransUnion's Forced Arbitration Terms of Service

HERE IS THE ONE TRANSUNION SNEAKES INTO THEIR TERMS OF USE:

AGREEMENT TO RESOLVE DISPUTES BY BINDING INDIVIDUAL ARBITRATION

THIS SECTION IS AN AGREEMENT TO ARBITRATE DISPUTES ("ARBITRATION AGREEMENT") THAT MAY ARISE AS A RESULT OF YOUR TRANSUNION INTERACTIVE MEMBERSHIPS, PRODUCTS OR SERVICES OR THE AGREEMENT. READ THIS SECTION CAREFULLY. YOU UNDERSTAND AND AGREE THAT BOTH PARTIES WOULD HAVE HAD A RIGHT TO LITIGATE DISPUTES THROUGH A COURT AND TO HAVE A JUDGE OR JURY DECIDE THEIR CASE, BUT BOTH PARTIES BY ENTERING INTO THIS AGREEMENT CHOOSE TO HAVE ANY DISPUTE RESOLVED THROUGH BINDING INDIVIDUAL ARBITRATION. OTHER RIGHTS THAT YOU WOULD HAVE IF YOU WENT TO COURT MAY NOT BE AVAILABLE OR MAY BE MORE LIMITED IN ARBITRATION, INCLUDING YOUR RIGHT TO APPEAL.

RIGHT TO REJECT ARBITRATION

YOU HAVE THE RIGHT TO REJECT THIS ARBITRATION AGREEMENT, BUT YOU MUST EXERCISE THIS RIGHT PROMPTLY. You must notify us in writing within sixty (60) days after the date you click-on to "Accept" the Agreement. You must send your request to: TransUnion Interactive, 100 Cross Street, Suite 202, San Luis Obispo, CA 93401. This request must include your current username and a clear statement of your intent, such as "I reject the arbitration clause in the TransUnion Interactive Service Agreement."

Opt Out of Forced Arbitration

Professional Driver Reveals Rapid Credit Repair System

If you need help go to my website:

UrbanCreditSecrets.com or email me at

UrbanCreditRepairSolutions@gmail.com   Jason Kirkwood

Opt out now so you can go to jury if you have to. This also makes your threats to sue real. If you threaten to sue but haven't sent in your Opt out letter you do not have that option.

Here's what you need to do:
Send the letter I provided to you
Enclose the Identification Form
Have it notarized
Send it registered mail
Keep copies and keep the mailing receipt

Professional Driver Reveals Rapid Credit Repair System

Identification Form

Copy Driver's License

Bill addressed to you

Pay check stub with your address on it

On the bottom of this "ID DOCUMENT"

I declare under penalty of perjury (under the laws of the United States of America) that this identification provide is me
John Doe
Signature
Date

Opt Out Letter

Your Name
Address
City, State
Zip
SSN: 000-00-0000 | DOB: 1/1/1970
User ID:
(This is your user Id for your TransUnion or Equifax or Experian account)

CREDIT REPORTING AGENCY
PO BOX ADDRESS
CITY, STATE
ZIP CODE

I have recently purchase a credit report from (TransUnion Equifax Experian) Please use this written letter as confirmation that I hereby Opt out and do not wish to resolve disputes with Equifax through arbitration.

Again: I reject the arbitration clause in the TransUnion Interactive Service Agreement.

Thank you for noting my account.

{YOUR NAME HERE}
Signature:_____
Date: _____

IN WITNESS WHEREOF, the said party has signed and sealed these presents the day and year first above written. Signed, sealed and delivered in the presence of:
{PRINT   YOUR   NAME   HERE}
_____ Signature

Professional Driver Reveals Rapid Credit Repair System

STATE OF
COUNTY OF
I HEREBY CERTIFY that on this day before me, an officer duly qualified to take acknowledgments, personally appeared { YOUR NAME HERE }, who has produced _____ as identification and who executed the foregoing instrument and he/she acknowledged before me that he/she executed the same.

WITNESS my hand and official seal in the County and State aforesaid this _____ day of _____2016.

_____ Notary Public
Printed Name
My commission expires:

Now Get it Notarized

Now you need to get the letter(s) notarized. You will add a copy of your social security card and Driver License (or passport) for proof of your identity and go a notary of the public. DO NOT SIGN THE LETTERS UNTIL YOU GO TO THE NOTARY AND THEY TELL YOU TO SIGN IT.

Opt Out Addresses

You may opt-out by writing to

Experian Consumer Services
Attn.: Arbitration Opt-Out
475 Anton Boulevard,
Costa Mesa, CA 92626

Equifax Consumer Services LLC,
Attn.: Arbitration Opt-Out,
P.O. Box 105496,
Atlanta, GA 30348

TransUnion Interactive
Attn.: Arbitration Opt-Out,
100 Cross Street, Suite 202,
San Luis Obispo, CA 93401.

Now Track Your letters

Now your letters are ready to send. You will send your letter WITH TRACKING Priority Mail. This is your proof that CRA's get your letter(s).

This is an absolute must.

File all your paperwork.

Repairing your Credit Supplies

Preparing for the war. Here are the tools you will need:

1) **Pen**
2) **9 Folders**
3) **Paper**
4) **Access to a Printer**
5) **Access to reports in real time from creditkarma.com and Experian.com**
6) **30 Copies of Your Identification Form (page 101)**

Now when we say credit repair we are really talking about increasing your Fico score because that is the only important part of your credit.

Credit Repair Simplified

Here are the things we want to focus on:

1) Bankruptcy   Yes/No

2) Decrease your Credit utilization – "the amount you have borrowed compared to your credit limit" –This is a key ratio.

3) Add credit lines that report to the credit bureaus.

4) Add your utility bills

5) Add accounts to your reports that are in good standing.

6) Removing Adverse Items that not are yours.

7) Removing Adverse Items that are yours.

8) Be able to monitor everything from our credit monitoring.

Step 1: Do you declare Bankruptcy and be done with the whole thing.

The Basics of Credit Card Debt and Bankruptcy

In an economy where housing problems dominate the headlines, high interest credit cards still remain one of the largest issues consumers face in their fight for financial health. It should come as no surprise to learn then, that credit card debt is still one of the primary reasons consumers are forced to file for bankruptcy. When a credit card account has been delinquent for more than 180 days, banks will charge off what is owed as "bad debt" and sell the account to a debt collector who will call, harass and even sue if the past due balances are high enough. Mounting pressure from debt collectors pushes many consumers through the front door of a bankruptcy office because chapter 7 protection is widely perceived as the fastest and best way to get out from under unmanageable credit card debt. While it is true that filing for bankruptcy can help discharge credit card bills, there are some basics that every consumer needs to know before relying on bankruptcy as a debt relief measure.

In this post we will give you the basics so that you can evaluate whether bankruptcy is a good solution to your credit card problems. Please also be sure to browse the related posts section of this page for additional information.

Credit Card Debt is Dischargeable in Bankruptcy.

That's the number one rule when it comes to unsecured debts like credit

cards debts and medical bills, they are dischargeable in bankruptcy. When you file for bankruptcy, all of your unsecured debts are eliminated, meaning you do not legally owe these bills any longer. Credit card companies who choose to pursue you for old, discharged debts will do so in violation of the law and will be subject to sanctions by the bankruptcy court. Furthermore, unlike debts that are forgiven through private negotiation with a lender, there is no tax liability for debts that are discharged in bankruptcy.

Your Credit Reports Should Show ZERO Balances on Your Credit Cards After Bankruptcy.

This is an area where consumers get tripped up. After bankruptcy, The credit card companies are required to report discharged debt as having a ZERO balance. It is often necessary to check your credit report and confirm its accuracy after your case closes.

Fraud Will Prevent Credit Card Debt From Being Discharged

While the general rule is that credit card debt is easily eliminated by filing for bankruptcy, fraudulent activity can jeopardize your entire bankruptcy discharge. Using credit cards for luxury purchases prior to bankruptcy creates a presumption of fraud which can be difficult to overcome. Don't use credit cards after meeting with a bankruptcy attorney unless you've decided not to file. The bottom line is any use of credit cards with the intention of not paying the debt back is fraudulent. The bankruptcy code protects debtors who behave in good faith and punish debtors who to try to game the system. For more information see: Using Credit Cards Before Bankruptcy is a Big No No!

Can You Keep a Credit Card Out of Your Bankruptcy?

All debts including credit card debts, must be disclosed in your bankruptcy petition. This means that you cannot keep any credit card that has a balance "out of your bankruptcy", it must be disclosed and will be discharged along with the rest of your unsecured debts. Credit cards with zero balances do not create a debt obligation and are therefore not required to be disclosed in a bankruptcy filing. For more information see: Can I Keep a Credit Card Out of Bankruptcy?

Will I be Able to Get a Credit Card After Bankruptcy?

Professional Driver Reveals Rapid Credit Repair System

Believe it or not yes. Creditor companies often send debtors offers for credit cards after they filed for bankruptcy knowing that it will be 8 years before they can file for bankruptcy again. Additionally, bankruptcy will illuminate all of your unsecured debt making your debt to income ratio more attractive to lenders who see that you now have the ability to take on new debt. This is not to say that filing for bankruptcy is good for your credit, because it is not. However, consumers emerging from bankruptcy commonly receive offers for cards in the mail very soon after their bankruptcy case has closed.

The Bottom Line

the bottom line is that as long as you're acting good faith credit card debt will be discharged in a bankruptcy filing. In fact, one of the main reasons why consumers are forced into bankruptcy is high-interest credit card debt. If you're facing credit card bills that have spiraled out-of-control, it is never a bad idea to meet with a bankruptcy attorney to discuss your options.

As I said before BANKRUPTCY is a great way out.

Decrease your Credit Utilization

Credit use ratio accounts for 30 percent of your score

This is **SO IMPORTANT.** Here is how it works.

Now let's look a 2 different people

John Doe

Peter Smith

They have exactly the same items on their credit reports except

John has a credit card with a limit of $10,000 on it and owes $7000. He has a great job making $125,000 a year and pays on time every month.

Peter has the exact same items on his credit but he has a credit card from the same company but his limit is $1000 because he is unemployed. He owes $100 on it and pays on time every month.

If you need help go to my website:

UrbanCreditSecrets.com or email me at
UrbanCreditRepairSolutions@gmail.com   Jason Kirkwood

Who has a much better score?

Its Peter because of the Credit Utilization. He is only using 10% of his available credit.

While John is using 70%.

This is so important with your Fico Score. It means so much I have to stress this point. It makes up 30% or more of your score.

But in reality it can jump you from a 580 to a 680.

Credit Utilization Components

The credit utilization category has six subcomponents:

The amount of debt still owed to lenders.

The number of accounts with debt outstanding.

The amount of debt owed on individual accounts.

The lack of a certain type of loan, in some cases.

The percentage of credit lines in use on revolving accounts, like credit cards.

The percentage of debt still owed on installment loans, like mortgages.

It's the comparison of amount of debt to the credit limit that is crucial.

That ratio goes by several names -- credit utilization ratio, credit-limit-to-debt ratio, balance-to-limit ratio and debt-to-available-credit ratio among them

-- but the math is simple. It's the percentage of how much you owe compared to the amount of your credit limit. If you owe $100 on your credit card and have a $1,000 credit limit on it, your ratio is 10 percent.

Professional Driver Reveals Rapid Credit Repair System

Simple, right? Not always. Here's where it gets tricky:

First of all, FICO doesn't view all account types as being equal. "Revolving balances (e.g., credit and retail cards) tend to carry more weight than installment debt (e.g., mortgage, auto and student loans) when amounts owed are considered,"

That means that within the amounts owed category, credit cards are the most important type of account for achieving a high FICO score, but they can also do more damage than other types of credit.

Additionally, while you might consider closing an unused or unwanted credit card to be a smart financial decision, because of the way your utilization ratio is calculated, the FICO score doesn't see it that way.

As an example, imagine you have two credit cards, each with a $500 credit limit, for total available credit of $1,000.

One of the cards hasn't been used for a while and has a zero balance, while the other card has a balance of $250. That gives you a utilization ratio of 25 percent -- your $250 balance divided by your total $1,000 credit limit. You then close that unused card, eliminating the $500 credit limit associated with that account. Now, you've only got $500 in total credit available on that one card, but you still have $250 in debt.

Suddenly, your credit utilization ratio has jumped to 50 percent.

That change can drag down your FICO score -- despite your good intentions. People think closing your cards was always a good thing.

However, when it comes to credit scoring, "Common sense doesn't always work.

It's not only your own actions that can change that utilization ratio for the worse. The bank may also take steps that have a negative impact on a cardholder's FICO score.

Some people have seen a score go down because an issuer had cut a credit line or closed their card for nonuse.

As in the example above, those changes can make it look like the borrower is closer to maxing out their line of credit, which can weigh on a borrower's FICO score.

Ace your credit utilization

To improve the amounts owed portion of your FICO score, start by finding out how much credit you have available. Then, pay down balances. If you're a good customer, the banks may also grant requests to increase your revolving credit lines. An old rule of thumb used to say keep your credit utilization below 30 percent, but that's a myth. There's no magic about 30 percent. Your score won't plummet at 31 percent or soar at 29 percent. The real rule? The lower the utilization, the better.

That can be especially tough for borrowers who only have one account. "If you've got one credit card with a $1,000 line, it's not that hard to hit 30 percent," since you'd only need to carry a balance of $300.

But if you max out a credit card account by using up an entire line of credit, expect your FICO score to drop by 10 to 45 points.

Another danger comes from joint account holders or authorized users who put excessive charges on your shared card. If the other cardholder maxes out a shared account, your FICO score may fall.

Another recommendation? Consider making payments to creditors more than once each month. Otherwise, if you put a major expense -- like a new appliance -- on a credit card, even if you plan to pay it off, your FICO score may take a hit. The reason is that credit scores are calculated as a snapshot in time, so if that happens to be right after you charged a new $700 washing machine, your utilization ratio will look worryingly high.

Things to do to for Best Credit Utilization

It's all about the credit cards.

If you have a credit card you don't use, start using it a little. Around 10% of the limit.

Call all your credit card companies and ask for a large increase to your limit.

Pay your credit cards down to 10% with a loan against your house. If you have equity in your home get a Home Equity Line of Credit.

A home equity line of credit (often called HELOC and pronounced Hee-lock) is a loan in which the lender agrees to lend a maximum amount within an agreed period (called a term), where the collateral is the borrower's equity in his/her house (akin to a second mortgage).

The rates for these are extremely low.

Your credit will sky rocket.

Go to : lendingtree.com and shop for the best rate.

Now let's say you are buying a house and have $25,000 down and have credit cards that are maxed out with $5000 limit.

You are ten times better to pay your cards down to $500.

Put down $20,500 on house instead. Your Fico will sky rocket and you will get a much better interest rate.

Whatever you do get your card balances low. Everyone can smell a dying fish.

Add credit lines that report to the credit bureaus.

This goes hand and hand with credit utilization because it decrease your debt load.

First check your creditkarma.com for "recommendations". These will always be cards that you are approved for based on your credit score.

Apply for all the cards they show. You will be approved.

Go to creditcards.com and apply for cards for bad credit.

Add Secured Credit Lines that Report to the Credit Bureaus.

What is a Secured Line

The biggest difference between a secured and an unsecured credit

card is that secured cards typically require a security deposit from the cardholder, which functions as cash collateral against you defaulting on your payments.

Secured credit cards are especially useful for consumers with poor or little to no credit history who are typically declined for unsecured credit cards. A secured card can almost guarantee approval by the lending institution because, in effect, you are the one taking on the financial risk through your security deposit.

Think of a secured card as your credit line "training wheels" that allow you the benefits of owning a credit card while giving you the opportunity to build a history of responsible credit use with on-time payments. The small credit limits and security deposit requirements are there to protect you from getting yourself into the poor payment history that may have plagued you in the past.

Secured card credit limits are often set at the amount of the security deposit or some percentage of it so that you cannot charge more than your security deposit can cover. Depending on your specific secured card, adding more to your security deposit enables you to access a higher credit limit, or if your payments are on-time and consistent, the credit card company may reward you by increasing your credit line without requiring additional deposits.

Many secured cards increase the credit limit of your secured card after 6-12 months of responsible use and on-time payments.

Get a Piggy Back Account

A "piggybacker," more commonly known as an "authorized user," is a person permitted to use a credit card by a primary cardholder who maintains responsibility for all debt on the card, regardless of who makes the charges. Authorized users are typically -- though not always, as you'll see -- a spouse, partner, child, relative or friend of the primary account holder.

The term "piggybacking" refers to the way in which the entire credit history of an account is not only included in the primary cardholder's credit report and score, but also becomes part of the authorized user's report and score. this happens whether the card is actually used by the authorized user or not.

In recent years, piggybacking has become one of the more popular, and at the same time controversial, ways of building credit for someone who is either new to credit or recovering from financial setbacks. Popular, due to the ease with which an authorized user can be added to an account -- no credit requirements -- and the immediate scoring benefit that can be realized from the primary cardholder's (hopefully) positive credit history. Controversial, in that someone who has not used, not managed, or has even misused credit in the past, can reap the scoring benefit of a seasoned and well-managed card without having truly done anything to earn the additional scoring points that can accompany the account. For example, a young person piggybacking on a parent's long-held and well maintained card can, without having any credit of her own, achieve a very good credit score based on a credit history older than she!

But, the piggybacking picture is not all win-win for authorized users.

Since the card history -- good or bad -- is included in the authorized user's credit report and credit score, it behooves the authorized user to make sure the card is always paid on time and maintains low credit utilization (card balance/limit percentage). Otherwise, piggybacking could backfire and result in a worse credit score than you'd have without being an authorized user on the card. In fact, consider this to be just one more of the many good reasons to check your credit reports.

Fortunately, should you discover that the primary account holder is not managing the account to your liking, you can have yourself removed from the account -- preferably by having the primary account holder contact the lender -- and have it removed from your credit report by disputing it as "not mine" with the credit bureaus.

Perhaps the most controversial aspect of piggybacking in recent years has been the use of this feature to artificially inflate credit scores for profit via a purely business-only relationship in which the piggybacker, often a complete stranger, pays to be added as an authorized user without receiving a card or participating in the managing the account in any way.

In an attempt to head off such piggybacking abuse, the FICO 8 credit score, launched in 2009, initially excluded accounts held as an authorized user from scoring. FICO quickly reversed course, however,

and went back to allowing piggybacking in scores -- but with an adjustment to generate fewer points for accounts held as an authorized user than as a primary account holder. It had become apparent to FICO that the price for discouraging piggybacking abuse by a relative few would be the denial of honestly-earned credit history for millions of legitimate authorized users -- most often the spouses of primary cardholders -- who use and manage these accounts no differently than those in the primary role.

You should consider the authorized user option as an easy-to-implement, minimal-risk way to build or rebuild credit

Add Your Utilities and Rent

Now you can't actually add your utility bills and rent to your Fico but you can add it to your PRBC score which you can show lenders.

Before you take out a loan or make a big purchase, lenders will want to be sure you'll make your payments. Having a good credit score tells them you're reliable. The trouble is, traditional scores don't include some of your most important payment habits. That means you could be paying all of your bills on time, every month, but still be denied a loan. With PRBC, those "other" bill payments are part of the decision.

To get a PRBC Score and Report, become a member and register at least three monthly-billed accounts. These might be your rent, your electric bill, your cable bill or even an online service. Then, all you have to do is be sure to pay your bills on time every month. When you do, your good habits show up as a good PRBC Score.

The more accounts you add, and keep up your payments on, the higher your PRBC Score will go. And best of all, getting started on the road to better credit is absolutely free.

You can do this at:
www.prbc.com

Professional Driver Reveals Rapid Credit Repair System

Add All Your Good Standing Accounts

Now check all your reports and make sure all off your reports are showing all your good accounts.

Your good accounts might only be showing on one or two bureau's.

If you find any of these accounts here is how to add the good account.

Enclose any documentation that verifies information you're providing.

Sample Add Account Letter

To Whom It May Concern

,According to the Fair Credit Reporting Act, 15 USC section 1681i, I request that you add the following credit accounts to my credit report:

Company Name
: [Name of Company]

Account Number
: [Account Number]

Account Type
: [Account Type]

Phone Number
: [Phone Number]

Date
: [Date]

I appreciate your attention to this matter, Please inform me within the statutory 30-day time period from your receipt of The purpose of this credit repair letter of your compliance with the provisions described in 15 USC 1681e,which require that all information in a consumer's credit report must reflect the maximum possible level of accuracy".

[Name]
Social Security Number: [Social Security Number]
Date of Birth: [Date of Birth]

Professional Driver Reveals Rapid Credit Repair System

If you need help go to my website:

UrbanCreditSecrets.com or email me at

UrbanCreditRepairSolutions@gmail.com   Jason Kirkwood

[Current Address]:[City, State Zip]Sincerely,

[Signature]
[Date
IN WITNESS WHEREOF, the said party has signed and sealed these presents the day and year first above written. Signed, sealed and delivered in the presence of:
{PRINT   YOUR   NAME   HERE}
_____ Signature
STATE OF
COUNTY OF
I HEREBY CERTIFY that on this day before me, an officer duly qualified to take acknowledgments, personally appeared
{   YOUR   NAME   HERE   },   who   has   produced
_____ as identification
and who executed the foregoing instrument and he/she acknowledged before me that he/she executed the same.
WITNESS my hand and official seal in the County and State aforesaid this _____ day of _____2016.

_____ Notary Public
Printed Name
My commission expires:

Add Your Identification Form to the letter Page 17

Now Get it Notarized

Now you need to get the letter(s) notarized.   You will add a copy of your social security card and Driver License (or passport) for proof of your identity and go a notary of the public. DO NOT SIGN THE LETTERS UNTIL YOU GO TO THE NOTARY AND THEY TELL YOU TO SIGN IT.

Now Track Your letters

Professional Driver Reveals Rapid Credit Repair System

Now your letters are ready to send. You will send your letter WITH TRACKING Certified Mail. This is your proof that CRA's get your letter(s).

This is an absolute must.

File all your paperwork

Here are the addresses you need to send the letters.

Equifax
P.O. Box 740256 Atlanta, GA 30374-0256
Experian
P.O. Box 2106 Allen, TX 75013
TransUnion
P.O. Box 34012 Fullerton, CA 92634

Make sure your address and employer are the same that the credit bureau has for you.

If this information is not correct change it on your credit report.

Login to your credit karma and Experian account and update your personal information. Make sure its updated before you send your letters. They are usually very quick with personal information updates.

Deleting Items From Your Report

Reports Have Errors

79 percent of all credit reports contain some type of error - and 25 percent contain such serious errors that those individuals could be denied credit.

Here are other significant findings:

54 percent contained inaccurate personal information such as misspelled names, wrong Social Security numbers, inaccurate birth dates, inaccurate information about a spouse and out of date address. For example, one credit report listed a man's business partner as his spouse.

If you need help go to my website:

UrbanCreditSecrets.com or email me at
UrbanCreditRepairSolutions@gmail.com   Jason Kirkwood

30 percent listed "closed" accounts as "open." For example, listing a student loan that was paid off years ago as still outstanding. Another report listed several credit cards, a mortgage and an auto loan all as open.

22 percent of reports had the same mortgage or loan listed twice. This mistake often occurs when loans are serviced or sold.

8 percent of reports simply didn't list major credit, loan, mortgage or other accounts that could be used to demonstrate the creditworthiness of a consumer.

These errors can create the appearance of a consumer having "too much" credit available, being over-extended, or not having been a responsible payer of his or her obligations.

The "big three" credit report bureaus - Equifax, Experian and TransUnion - have been in this business for years, so how can they possibly be making all of these mistakes?

Most mistakes can be pinned to your creditors and others providing info to the credit bureaus. As mentioned above, some mistakes happen when credit accounts change hands. Some errors are intentional. The report found that some banks admit to not furnishing bureaus with complete information on customers.

Other mistakes are simply human error. According to a credit bureau industry spokesman, some 30,000 data processors file 4.5 billion updates to credit reports each month, leaving considerable room for errors.

These errors on credit reports can cause consumers serious trouble. Many consumers probably don't realize just how serious.

Are the Debts Yours?

Now make sure they are actually not your debts. This is important just so you know who you are dealing with.

For example all creditors sell their debts to third parties. So Here is a debt showing up on a TransUnion credit report:

Professional Driver Reveals Rapid Credit Repair System

Collection Account Example 1

Account Details
Last Reported

Apr 26, 2015

Collection Agency

ERC

Original Creditor

11 AT T

Status

Open

Opened Date

Mar 09, 2015

Closed Date

--

Responsibility

Individual

Balance

$59

High Balance

$59

Remarks

Placed for collection

Creditor Contact Details
ENHANCED RECOVERY COMPAN
PO BOX 57547
JACKSONVILLE, FL
32241
(800) 496-8941

NOW YOU DON'T KNOW THE COMPANY "ENHANCED RECOVERY COMPANY
BUT IF YOU SEE THE ORIGINAL DEBTOR IS AT&T YOU MIGHT KNOW THEM.

Collection Account Example 2

CMRE FINANCIAL SERVICES

MED1 02 MEDICAL PAYMENT DATA

Jul 17, 2014
Open

$472

Account Details
Last Reported

Nov 21, 2015

Collection Agency

CMRE FINANCIAL SERVICES

Original Creditor

MED1 02 MEDICAL PAYMENT DATA

Status

Open

Opened Date

Jul 17, 2014

Closed Date

--

Responsibility

Individual

Balance

$472

High Balance

$416

Remarks

Placed for collection

Creditor Contact Details
CMRE FINANCIAL SERVICES
3075 E IMPERIAL HW 200

Professional Driver Reveals Rapid Credit Repair System

BREA, CA
92821
(877) 572-7555

Now the original creditor here is CMRE FINANCIAL SERVICES. They are not a company that is easily recognized but you might have had a service done. In this case it was an X-Ray.

Setting up Your Folders Like This:

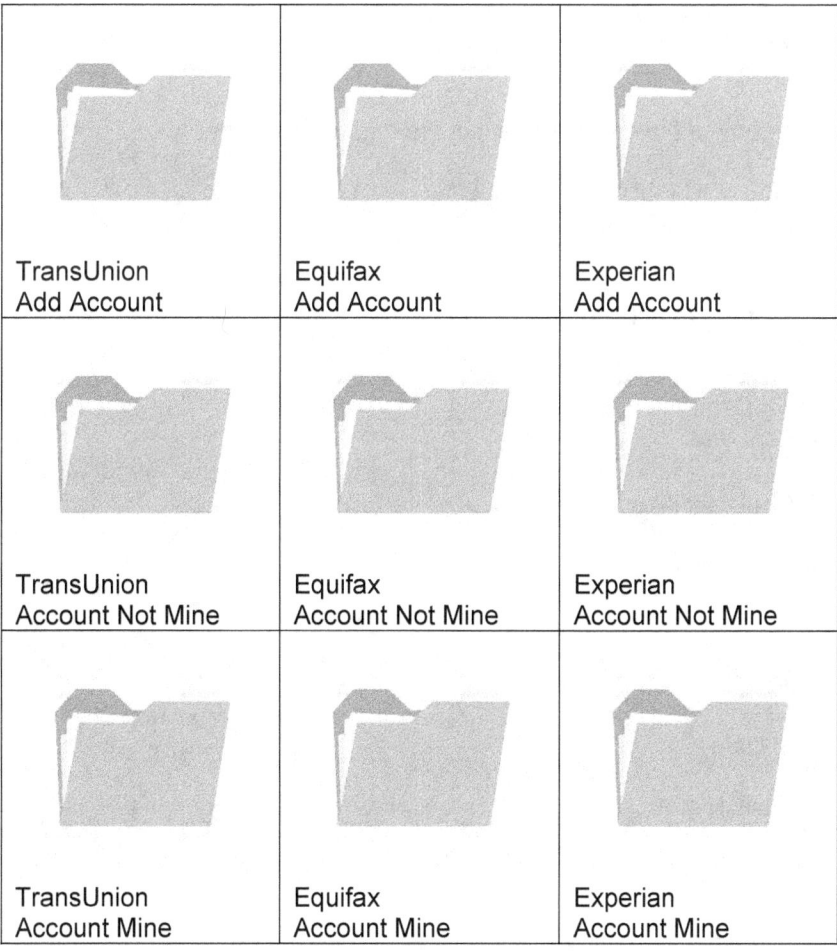

TransUnion Add Account	Equifax Add Account	Experian Add Account
TransUnion Account Not Mine	Equifax Account Not Mine	Experian Account Not Mine
TransUnion Account Mine	Equifax Account Mine	Experian Account Mine

Add Account folder is for accounts you want to add.
Accounts Not Mine are accounts you don't believe are yours. Look into these accounts before you file them in this folder.
Accounts Mine are accounts you recognize but want to delete anyway.

Print a Copy of all Accounts on Your Credit Reports
That You are Going to Add or Dispute

Print a copy of the debt and file it in the appropriate folder.

BEFORE YOU FILE THE DEBT CALL AND GET THE ACCOUNT NUMBER.

So with this example debt

Account Details
Last Reported

Apr 26, 2015

Collection Agency

ERC

Original Creditor

411 AT T

Status

Open

Opened Date

Mar 09, 2015

Closed Date

--

Responsibility

Individual

Balance

$59

High Balance

$59

Remarks

Professional Driver Reveals Rapid Credit Repair System

Creditor Contact Details
ENHANCED RECOVERY COMPAN
PO BOX 57547
JACKSONVILLE, FL
32241
(800) 496-8941

First you should call ATT

If that doesn't work you would call:

Creditor Contact Details
ENHANCED RECOVERY COMPAN
PO BOX 57547
JACKSONVILLE, FL
32241
(800) 496-8941

Sample Call to Original Creditor

Your phone call should go like this: Hello I saw this debt on my credit report that I'm not sure is mine. If it is mine I am willing to pay it. What is the account number from the AT&T account so I can check my records. My social # is 645-98-9876.

After you get the account number for the original debt write it on your debt page.

Sample Call to Collection Company

THE COLLECTION COMPANY.   BLOCK YOUR PHONE NUMBER. You don't want them calling you. Do not give them information but get the account# for the original debt if you don't know it.

Your phone call should go like this: Hello I saw this debt on my credit report that I'm not sure is mine. If it is mine I am willing to pay it. What is the account number from the AT&T account so I can check my records.

Many times they will say your account number is not with AT&T anymore It's with them, don't take that answer. You need the account number for the original creditor because you don't want to pay someone

else's debt.

After you get the account number for the original debt write it on your debt page.

Make sure you check with AT&T that the number they gave you is an account number with them.

The Secret to Disputing Accounts

What you should have done

9 Folders
Experian-Add Account
Experian-Account Not Mine
Experian-Account Mine

Equifax-Add Account
Equifax-Account Not Mine
Equifax-Account Mine

TransUnion-Add Account
TransUnion-Not Mine
TransUnion-Account Mine

You should now have a printed a copy of all your debts with the original account number. You should also have accounts you want to add.

If you haven't don't have these things done go back and do them. This is absolutely necessary.

Never Dispute Things Online

I NEED TO SAY THIS AGAIN AND AGAIN NEVER DISPUTE ANYTHING ONLINE.

3 Reasons You Should Never Dispute Credit Errors Online

Professional Driver Reveals Rapid Credit Repair System

Reason Number One: Time

One important factor you have on your side when disputing errors in your credit report is time. By law, the credit bureaus have 30 days within receipt of that dispute to properly investigate your claim. However, this only applies to reports other than one obtained for free at annualcreditreport.com. In that case, the credit bureaus have 45 days to respond.

Like I told you before don't get your report from annualcreditreport.com

Reason Number Two: Shortcut The Process

The Credit Bureaus online dispute system is set up in such a way that when you use it, it makes their job that much easier. The information you put into their limited dispute fields falls right into their electronic verification system. By using their online dispute system (E-OSCAR), **you have no proof of the dispute or a paper trail that certified return receipt requested would give you if you had mailed that dispute.** An important aspect of accelerating the credit recovery process is keeping meticulous records.

If you catch the credit bureaus in violation of the Fair Credit Reporting Act or a collection company in violation of the Fair Debt Collection Practices Act, you'll have the necessary ammunition to beat them in court and clear your good name should you have to go that route.

Reason Number Three: Revision Not In Your Favor

When the Fair Credit Reporting Act was revised by FACTA, they put in a section for "Expedited Dispute Resolution" Section 611a(8), also known as the on-line dispute system. If you read this section, you will notice the following;

Well paragraph 2 is the part that requires the CRA to forward your dispute and all related documentation you provide to the creditor or company furnishing the information to the bureau. Paragraph 6 is the part that requires the CRA to provide you with written results of the re-investigation. And paragraph 7 is the part that requires the CRA to provide you with the method of verification on request by you, the consumer.

So as you can see, by using the CRA'S online disputing system (E-OSCAR), which by the way stands for Electronic Online System for

Complete and Accurate Reporting (lol), you wouldn't receive a notice from the credit bureaus telling you that the information you disputed has been verified as accurate, which, by receiving this notice is what allows you to request the method of verification (MOV). The credit bureau then must provide you with this information within 15 days of your request.

Important Tool

As you can see, Method of Verification is another important tool to use and a very important part of accelerating the process of credit recovery should you need to delete an item discovered to be in error, incomplete, or unverifiable during the "Credit Audit and Verification" process.   So why would you give these rights up; voluntarily no less?

Additionally, the law is not specific enough and does not say "permanently delete or suppress"; herein lays the problem. The Credit Reporting Agencies (CRA) can "soft delete" a disputed trade line for 30 days and then the trade line can reappear when the furnisher (creditor or collector) reports it again in the next 30 day cycle. This is due to the fact that the CRA's are not required to tell the creditor or collector that you disputed it at all, thanks to the "shall not be required to comply with paragraphs 2" if you decide to dispute an item online. Are you getting all of this?

This is a deceptive system in where you, the Amateur Consumer, think you may have succeeded in your dispute and gotten what is known as a "hard delete", but in fact, it is only temporary. Since the creditor or furnisher of that information does not know the item was deleted, they will mistakenly re-report it and then conveniently, the credit bureau will place the negative item back on your report. And if that isn't bad enough, you lose the hard copy of the investigation results you would otherwise have received and been entitled to if the dispute had been sent via certified mail in the first place.

Again, by disputing in writing, as the FTC states you should on their website, the bureaus might temporarily remove a negative item (soft delete) until the information is verified as true but…if the information is verified to be true, they must then notify you in writing within 5 days of putting the item back on your credit report. If they don't, it's a violation of the FCRA and you could potentially sue them for $1,000.

Professional Driver Reveals Rapid Credit Repair System

Listen To The FTC

Look, there's a reason why the FTC states right there on its website that you should dispute EVERY item you think is not accurate, incomplete, or unverifiable on your credit in writing and by certified mail, "return receipt requested"; it's because you are protected as a consumer and by disputing online electronically, you lose many rights under FCRA. So why would you ever do this

Two Means of Disputes

1) Disputing with the credit bureau.
2) Disputing with the collection company/original debtor

You have rights in both these situations. Let's get ready to remove those negative items.

Disputing with the Credit Bureaus

Many of the adverse items on a credit report may in fact be true.

So, if you were to dispute the adverse items with a traditional dispute process most of those accounts will be "verified" and will stay on your credit report thus in turn keeping your FICO score down.

That is NOT what you are going to do.

SECTION 609 of the Fair Credit Reporting Act does not care whether the negative account is valid or not. The letter disputes the CRA's right to REPORT the adverse account –

NOT whether or not the adverse account is valid. These letters will request, under SECTION 609 of the Fair Credit Reporting Act, that the CRA's send you a copy of the original contract that you signed – that they are supposed to have.

If they are verifying the account as being valid/correct then they, by law, are supposed to have a copy of that contract to do so. THEY DON'T. And since they don't they can't provide you a copy nor can they

legally verify the account.

Under the Fair Credit Reporting Act they must provide you a copy if you request it.   Since they will not be able to provide you such a document the account will be UNVERIFIED and under Federal Law any UNVERIFIED accounts must be deleted.

Disputing with the Bureaus Must Do's

1) First you should hand write all your letters ok I know this seems like a lot of work but it's worth it. You have to be the customer who is really disputing an item. You are not using a website template. You have hand written your letters.

2) All Letters have to be notarized.

3) All letters have to be sent registered mail.

4) All letters have to include your "Identification Form"

5) Dispute 2 items with each bureau at a time.

Dispute Addresses

Experian's mailing address for dispute requests is:
P.O. Box 4500
Allen, TX 75013

Equifax Information Services LLC
P.O. Box 740256
Atlanta, GA 30374

TransUnion Consumer Solutions
P.O. Box 2000
Chester, PA 19022-2000

Always mail to these addresses.

Include this form with letters to Equifax

Professional Driver Reveals Rapid Credit Repair System

http://www.equifax.com/cp/MailInDislcosureRequest.pdf

Include this form with letters to TransUnion
www.transunion.com/docs/rev/personal/InvestigationRequest.pdf

GENERATION 1.0 LETTER

Your Name
Address
City, State
Zip
SSN: 000-00-0000 | DOB: 1/1/1970

Experian
P.O. Box 4500
Allen, TX 75013

According to the Fair Credit Reporting Section 609 (a)(1)(A), you are required by federal law to verify - through the physical verification of the original signed consumer contract - any and all accounts you post on a credit report.

Otherwise, anyone paying for your reporting services could fax, mail or email in a fraudulent account. I demand to see Verifiable Proof (an original Consumer Contract with my Signature on it) you have on file of the accounts listed below.

Your failure to positively verify these accounts has hurt my ability to obtain credit.

Under the FCRA, unverified accounts must be removed and if you are unable to provide me a copy of verifiable proof, you must remove the accounts listed below.

I demand the following accounts be verified or removed immediately.
Account 1 (AT&T) _____ Account #_____
Account 1 (SPRINT) _____ Account #_____

Please note that I have opted out in writing to your forced arbitration terms and am willing to seek legal relief.
{Print Name}
{Signature}
{Date}

IN WITNESS WHEREOF, the said party has signed and sealed these presents the day and year first above written. Signed, sealed and delivered in the presence of:

Professional Driver Reveals Rapid Credit Repair System

If you need help go to my website:

UrbanCreditSecrets.com or email me at
UrbanCreditRepairSolutions@gmail.com   Jason Kirkwood

{PRINT   YOUR   NAME   HERE}
_____ Signature

STATE OF
COUNTY OF
I HEREBY CERTIFY that on this day before me, an officer duly qualified to take acknowledgments, personally appeared
{   YOUR   NAME   HERE   },   who   has   produced
_____ as identification and who executed the foregoing instrument and he/she acknowledged before me that he/she executed the same.

WITNESS my hand and official seal in the County and State aforesaid this _____ day of _____2016.

_____ Notary Public
Printed Name
My commission expires:

Professional Driver Reveals Rapid Credit Repair System

Identification Form GENERATION 1.0 LETTER

On the bottom of this "ID DOCUMENT"

I declare under penalty of perjury (under the laws of the United States of America) that this identification provide is me
John Doe

If you need help go to my website:

UrbanCreditSecrets.com or email me at

UrbanCreditRepairSolutions@gmail.com   Jason Kirkwood

Signature
Date

Now your letter is ready to send. You will send your letter WITH TRACKING Priority Mail. This is your proof that CRA's get your letter(s).

This is an absolute must.

File all your paperwork.
Possible Results

When you send your notarized letters to Equifax, TransUnion, and Experian they might try to ignore you.

They might send you a reply saying a suspicious letter was sent on your behalf but has been ignored or may try to intimidate you to stop you from continuing your disputes.

Here are some responses.

"We received a suspicious request regarding your personal credit information that we have determined was not sent by you. We have not taken any action on this request and any future requests made in this manner will not be processed and will not receive a response."

You might also get something like this: "Suspicious requests are taken seriously and reviewed by security personnel who will report deceptive activity, including copies of letters deemed as suspicious, to law enforcement officials and to state or federal regulatory agencies.

Professional Driver Reveals Rapid Credit Repair System

They may also ask for proof of your identity and request you mail them such proof.

You have already sent a notarized letter identification form with "I declare under penalty of perjury (under the laws of the United States of America) that this identification provide is me"

All these responses are great for you. They show that the bureaus are not providing information required and the timeline is ticking.

They are trying to scare you.

They can't do anything to you.

Repeat after me.

They can't scare me.
I will persist and prevail.

They can't scare me.
I will persist and prevail.

They can't scare me.
I will persist and prevail.

GENERATION 2.0 LETTER

Your Name
Address
City, State
Zip
SSN: 000-00-0000 | DOB: 1/1/1970

Experian
P.O. Box 4500
Allen, TX 75013

According to the Fair Credit Reporting Section 609 (a)(1)(A), you are required by federal law to verify - through the physical verification of the original signed consumer contract - any and all accounts you post on a credit report.

Otherwise, anyone paying for your reporting services could fax, mail or email in a fraudulent account. I demand to see Verifiable Proof (an original Consumer Contract with my Signature on it) you have on file of the accounts listed below.

Your failure to positively verify these accounts has hurt my ability to obtain credit.

Under the FCRA, unverified accounts must be removed and if you are unable to provide me a copy of verifiable proof, you must remove the accounts listed below. I demand the following accounts be verified or removed immediately.

Account 1 (AT&T) _____   Account #_____
Account 1 (SPRINT) _____   Account #_____

Please note that I have opted out in writing to your forced arbitration terms and am willing to seek legal relief.

Professional Driver Reveals Rapid Credit Repair System

{Print Name}
{Signature}
{Date}
IN WITNESS WHEREOF, the said party has signed and sealed these presents the day and year first above written. Signed, sealed and delivered in the presence of:
{PRINT   YOUR   NAME   HERE}
_____ Signature
STATE OF
COUNTY OF
I HEREBY CERTIFY that on this day before me, an officer duly qualified to take acknowledgments, personally appeared
{   YOUR   NAME   HERE   },   who   has   produced
_____ as identification
and who executed the foregoing instrument and he/she acknowledged before me that he/she executed the same.

WITNESS my hand and official seal in the County and State aforesaid this _____ day of _____2016.

_____ Notary Public
Printed Name
My commission expires:

Identification Form GENERATION 2.0 LETTER

Professional Driver Reveals Rapid Credit Repair System

On the bottom of this "ID DOCUMENT"

I declare under penalty of perjury (under the laws of the United States of America) that this identification provide is me
John Doe
Signature
Date

Now your letter is ready to send. You will send your letter WITH TRACKING Priority Mail. This is your proof that CRA's get your letter(s).

This is an absolute must. File all your paperwork.

Professional Driver Reveals Rapid Credit Repair System

If you need help go to my website:

UrbanCreditSecrets.com or email me at

UrbanCreditRepairSolutions@gmail.com   Jason Kirkwood

GENERATION 3.0 LETTER

Your Name
Address
City, State
Zip
SSN: 000-00-0000 | DOB: 1/1/1970

Experian
P.O. Box 4500
Allen, TX 75013

Please be advised this is my **THIRD WRITTEN REQUEST** and **FINAL WARNING** that I fully intend to pursue litigation in accordance with the FCRA to enforce my rights and seek relief and recover all monetary damages that I may be entitled to under Section 616 and Section 617 regarding your continued willful and negligent noncompliance.

Despite two written requests, the unverified items listed below still remain on my credit report in violation of Federal Law.

You are required under the FCRA to have a copy of the original creditors documentation on file to verify that this information is mine and is correct.

In the results of your first investigation and subsequent reinvestigation, you stated in writing that you "verified" that these items are being "reported correctly" ?

Who verified these accounts?   You have **NOT** provided me a copy of **ANY** original documentation (a consumer contract with my signature on it) as required under Section 609 (a)(1)(A) & Section 611 (a)(1)(A).

Furthermore you have failed to provide the method of verification as required under Section 611 (a) (7).

Please be advised that under Section 611 (5)(A) of the FCRA – you are required to "...promptly DELETE all information which cannot be verified."

The law is very clear as to the Civil liability and the remedy available to me (Section 616 & 617) if you fail to comply with Federal Law. I am a litigious consumer and fully intend on pursuing litigation in this matter to enforce my rights under the FCRA.

Account 1 (AT&T) _____ Account #_____
Account 1 (SPRINT) _____ Account #_____

Please note that I have opted out in writing to your forced arbitration terms and am willing to seek legal relief.

{Print Name}
{Signature}
{Date}

IN WITNESS WHEREOF, the said party has signed and sealed these presents the day and year first above written. Signed, sealed and delivered in the presence of:
{PRINT   YOUR   NAME   HERE}
_____ Signature
STATE OF
COUNTY OF
I HEREBY CERTIFY that on this day before me, an officer duly qualified to take acknowledgments, personally appeared
{   YOUR   NAME   HERE   },   who   has   produced
_____ as identification and who executed the foregoing instrument and he/she acknowledged before me that he/she executed the same.
WITNESS my hand and official seal in the County and State aforesaid this _____ day of _____2016.

_____ Notary Public
Printed Name
My commission expires:

--------------------End of Letter.

Professional Driver Reveals Rapid Credit Repair System

If you need help go to my website:

UrbanCreditSecrets.com or email me at
UrbanCreditRepairSolutions@gmail.com   Jason Kirkwood

Identification Form GENERATION 3.0 LETTER

Copy Driver's License

Bill addressed to you

Pay check stub with your address on it

Professional Driver Reveals Rapid Credit Repair System

On the bottom of this   "ID DOCUMENT"

I declare under penalty of perjury (under the laws of the United States of America) that this identification provide is me
John Doe
Signature
Date

Now your letter is ready to send. You will send your letter WITH TRACKING Priority Mail. This is your proof that CRA's get your letter(s).

This is an absolute must.

File all your paperwork.

Professional Driver Reveals Rapid Credit Repair System

If you need help go to my website:

UrbanCreditSecrets.com or email me at
UrbanCreditRepairSolutions@gmail.com   Jason Kirkwood

GENERATION 4.0 LETTER

Your Name
Address
City, State
Zip
SSN: 000-00-0000 | DOB: 1/1/1970

Experian
P.O. Box 4500
Allen, TX 75013

NOTICE OF PENDING LITIGATION SEEKING RELIEF AND MONETARY DAMAGES UNDER FCRA SECTION 616 & SECTION 617 Please accept this final written OFFER OF SETTLEMENT BEFORE LITIGATION as my attempt to amicably resolve your continued violation of the Fair Credit Reporting Act regarding your refusal to delete UNVERIFIED information from my consumer file.

I intend to pursue litigation in accordance with the FCRA to seek relief and recover all monetary damages that I may be entitled to under Section 616 and Section 617 if the UNVERIFIED items listed below are not deleted immediately.

A copy of this letter as well as copies of the three written letters sent to you previously will also become part of a formal complaint to the Federal Trade Commission and shall be used as evidence in pending litigation provided you fail to comply with this offer of settlement. Despite three written requests, the unverified items listed below still remain on my credit report in violation of Federal Law.

You are required under the FCRA to have a copy of the original creditors documentation on file to verify that this information is mine and is correct. In the results of your investigations, you stated in writing that you "verified" that these items are being "reported correctly"?   Who verified these accounts?

Professional Driver Reveals Rapid Credit Repair System

You have NOT provided me a copy of ANY original documentation (a consumer contract with my signature on it) as required under Section 609 (a)(1)(A) & Section 611 (a)(1)(A).

Furthermore you have failed to provide the method of verification as required under Section 611 (a) (7). Please be advised that under Section 611 (5)(A) of the FCRA – you are required to "…promptly DELETE all information which cannot be verified."

The law is very clear as to the Civil liability and the remedy available to me (Section 616 & 617) if you fail to comply with Federal Law. I am a litigious consumer and fully intend on pursuing litigation in this matter to enforce my rights under the FCRA.

Account 1 (AT&T) _____ Account #_____
Account 1 (SPRINT) _____ Account #_____

Please note that I have opted out in writing to your forced arbitration terms and am willing to seek legal relief.

{Print Name}
{Signature}
{Date}

IN WITNESS WHEREOF, the said party has signed and sealed these presents the day and year first above written. Signed, sealed and delivered in the presence of:
{PRINT   YOUR   NAME   HERE}
_____ Signature
STATE OF
COUNTY OF
I HEREBY CERTIFY that on this day before me, an officer duly qualified to take acknowledgments, personally appeared
{ YOUR NAME HERE }, who has produced
_____ as identification
and who executed the foregoing instrument and he/she acknowledged before me that he/she executed the same.

WITNESS my hand and official seal in the County and State aforesaid this _____ day of _____2016.

_____ Notary Public
Printed Name
My commission expires:

Professional Driver Reveals Rapid Credit Repair System

If you need help go to my website:

UrbanCreditSecrets.com or email me at
UrbanCreditRepairSolutions@gmail.com   Jason Kirkwood

--------------------End of Letter.

Identification Form GENERATION 4.0 LETTER

On the bottom of this   "ID DOCUMENT"

Professional Driver Reveals Rapid Credit Repair System

I declare under penalty of perjury (under the laws of the United States of America) that this identification provide is me
John Doe
Signature
Date

Now your letter is ready to send. You will send your letter WITH TRACKING Priority Mail. This is your proof that CRA's get your letter(s).

This is an absolute must.

File all your paperwork.

GENERATION 5.0 LETTER

Your Name
Address
City, State
Zip
SSN: 000-00-0000 | DOB: 1/1/1970

Experian
P.O. Box 4500
Allen, TX 75013

NOTICE OF PENDING LITIGATION SEEKING RELIEF AND
MONETARY DAMAGES UNDER FCRA SECTION 616 & SECTION 617
Please accept this final written OFFER OF SETTLEMENT BEFORE
LITIGATION as my attempt to amicably resolve your continued violation
of the Fair Credit Reporting Act regarding your refusal to delete
UNVERIFIED information from my consumer file.

I intend to pursue litigation in accordance with the FCRA to seek relief
and recover all monetary damages that I may be entitled to under
Section 616 and Section 617 if the UNVERIFIED items listed below are
not deleted immediately.

A copy of this letter as well as copies of the three written letters sent
to you previously will also become part of a formal complaint to the
Federal Trade Commission and shall be used as evidence in pending
litigation provided you fail to comply with this offer of settlement. Despite
three written requests, the unverified items listed below still remain on
my credit report in violation of Federal Law.

You are required under the FCRA to have a copy of the original
creditors documentation on file to verify that this information is mine and
is correct. In the results of your investigations, you stated in writing that
you "verified" that these items are being "reported correctly"?   Who
verified these accounts?
You have NOT provided me a copy of ANY original documentation (a

Professional Driver Reveals Rapid Credit Repair System

consumer contract with my signature on it) as required under Section 609 (a)(1)(A) & Section 611 (a)(1)(A).

Furthermore you have failed to provide the method of verification as required under Section 611 (a) (7).   Please be advised that under Section 611 (5)(A) of the FCRA – you are required to "…promptly DELETE all information which cannot be verified."

The law is very clear as to the Civil liability and the remedy available to me (Section 616 & 617) if you fail to comply with Federal Law. I am a litigious consumer and fully intend on pursuing litigation in this matter to enforce my rights under the FCRA.

Account 1 (AT&T) _____   Account #_____
Account 1 (SPRINT) _____   Account #_____

If I don't get proper documentation I will be filling my complaint at:
www.consumerfinance.gov/Complaint/
and
www.ftccomplaintassistant.gov/

Please note that I have opted out in writing to your forced arbitration terms and am willing to seek legal relief.

{Print Name}
{Signature}
{Date}

IN WITNESS WHEREOF, the said party has signed and sealed these presents the day and year first above written. Signed, sealed and delivered in the presence of:

{PRINT   YOUR   NAME   HERE}
_____ Signature

STATE OF
COUNTY OF

I HEREBY CERTIFY that on this day before me, an officer duly qualified to take acknowledgments, personally appeared
{   YOUR   NAME   HERE   },   who   has   produced
_____ as identification
and who executed the foregoing instrument and he/she acknowledged before me that he/she executed the same.

WITNESS my hand and official seal in the County and State aforesaid this _____ day of _____2016.

_____ Notary Public

 Professional Driver Reveals Rapid Credit Repair System

If you need help go to my website:

UrbanCreditSecrets.com or email me at
UrbanCreditRepairSolutions@gmail.com   Jason Kirkwood

Printed Name
My commission expires:

Identification Form GENERATION 5.0 LETTER

On the bottom of this   "ID DOCUMENT"

Professional Driver Reveals Rapid Credit Repair System

I declare under penalty of perjury (under the laws of the United States of America) that this identification provide is me
John Doe
Signature
Date

Now your letter is ready to send. You will send your letter WITH TRACKING Priority Mail. This is your proof that CRA's get your letter(s).

This is an absolute must.

File all your paperwork.

Small Claims Form Included

With this 6ᵗʰ letter enclose a copy of a small claims court filling. Fill it out completely like you are ready to file it.

Now don't actually file it just fill it out. You can get one for free at your local court house. Name the bureau as the defendant.

What you file against them for:

negligent and willful failure to provide - through the physical verification of the original signed consumer contract - any and all accounts you post on a credit report.
In violation Section 609 (a)(1)(A), FCRA

negligent and willful failure to reinvestigate the disputed entries in violation of sections 611(a), 616, and 617 of the FCRA, 15 U.S.C. §§ 1681i(a), 1681n, 1681o"

Professional Driver Reveals Rapid Credit Repair System

GENERATION 6.0 LETTER

Your Name
Address
City, State
Zip
SSN: 000-00-0000 | DOB: 1/1/1970

Experian
P.O. Box 4500
Allen, TX 75013

NOTICE OF PENDING LITIGATION SEEKING RELIEF AND MONETARY DAMAGES UNDER FCRA SECTION 616 & SECTION 617 Please accept this final written OFFER OF SETTLEMENT BEFORE LITIGATION as my attempt to amicably resolve your continued violation of the Fair Credit Reporting Act regarding your refusal to delete UNVERIFIED information from my consumer file.

I intend to pursue litigation in accordance with the FCRA to seek relief and recover all monetary damages that I may be entitled to under Section 616 and Section 617 if the UNVERIFIED items listed below are not deleted immediately.

A copy of this letter as well as copies of the three written letters sent to you previously will also become part of a formal complaint to the Federal Trade Commission and shall be used as evidence in pending litigation provided you fail to comply with this offer of settlement. Despite three written requests, the unverified items listed below still remain on my credit report in violation of Federal Law.

You are required under the FCRA to have a copy of the original creditors documentation on file to verify that this information is mine and is correct. In the results of your investigations, you stated in writing that you "verified" that these items are being "reported correctly"? Who verified these accounts?
You have NOT provided me a copy of ANY original documentation (a consumer contract with my signature on it) as required under Section 609 (a)(1)(A) & Section 611 (a)(1)(A).
Furthermore you have failed to provide the method of verification as required under Section 611 (a) (7). Please be advised that under

If you need help go to my website:

UrbanCreditSecrets.com or email me at

UrbanCreditRepairSolutions@gmail.com   Jason Kirkwood

Section 611 (5)(A) of the FCRA – you are required to "…promptly DELETE all information which cannot be verified."
    The law is very clear as to the Civil liability and the remedy available to me (Section 616 & 617) if you fail to comply with Federal Law. I am a litigious consumer and fully intend on pursuing litigation in this matter to enforce my rights under the FCRA.

       Account 1 (AT&T) _____ Account #_____
       Account 1 (SPRINT) _____ Account #_____

    If I don't get proper documentation I will be filling my complaint at:
    www.consumerfinance.gov/Complaint/
    and
    www.ftccomplaintassistant.gov/

    Please note that I have opted out in writing to your forced arbitration terms and am willing to seek legal relief.

    {Print Name}
    {Signature}
    {Date}

    IN WITNESS WHEREOF, the said party has signed and sealed these presents the day and year first above written. Signed, sealed and delivered in the presence of:
    {PRINT   YOUR   NAME   HERE}
_____ Signature
    STATE OF
    COUNTY OF
    I HEREBY CERTIFY that on this day before me, an officer duly qualified to take acknowledgments, personally appeared
    {   YOUR   NAME   HERE   },   who   has   produced
_____ as identification
and who executed the foregoing instrument and he/she acknowledged before me that he/she executed the same.
    WITNESS my hand and official seal in the County and State aforesaid this _____ day of _____2016.

Professional Driver Reveals Rapid Credit Repair System

_____ Notary Public
Printed Name
My commission expires:
Identification Form GENERATION 6.0 LETTER

Copy Driver's License

Bill addressed to you

Pay check stub with your address on it

On the bottom of this   "ID DOCUMENT"

I declare under penalty of perjury (under the laws of the United States of America) that this identification provide is me
John Doe
Signature
Date

Now your letter is ready to send. You will send your letter WITH TRACKING Priority Mail. This is your proof that CRA's get your letter(s).

This is an absolute must.

File all your paperwork.

Filling Your Complaint

You will have file complaint here:

www.consumerfinance.gov/Complaint/

scan all your documents sent to the bureaus and there responses. You will be able to upload them.

Disputing With The Original Debtor

BEFORE DISPUTING WITH THE ORIGINAL CREDITOR YOU MUST HAVE DISPUTED WITH THE CREDIT BUREAUS .

How to Dispute Listing with Original Creditor

Creditors are the companies who initially reported your account to the credit bureaus and many times they have no record of your account at all. By law they have to remove your account if this is the case and have no proof.

Here is the exact statute in the FCRA:

§ 623. (a)(8) ABILITY OF CONSUMER TO DISPUTE INFORMATION DIRECTLY WITH FURNISHER

(A) IN GENERAL The Federal banking agencies, the National Credit Union Administration, and the Commission shall jointly prescribe regulations that shall identify the circumstances under which a furnisher shall be required to reinvestigate a dispute concerning the accuracy of information contained in a consumer report on the consumer, based on a direct request of a consumer.

(B) CONSIDERATIONS - In prescribing regulations under subparagraph (A), the agencies shall weigh--

(i) the benefits to consumers with the costs on furnishers and the credit reporting system;

(ii) the impact on the overall accuracy and integrity of consumer reports of any such requirements;

(iii) whether direct contact by the consumer with the furnisher would likely result in the most expeditious resolution of any such dispute; and

(iv) the potential impact on the credit reporting process if credit repair organizations, as defined in section 403(3), including entities that would be a credit repair organization, but for section 403(3)(B)(i), are able to circumvent the prohibition in subparagraph (G).

(C) APPLICABILITY Subparagraphs (D) through (G) shall apply in any circumstance identified under the regulations promulgated under subparagraph (A).

(D) SUBMITTING A NOTICE OF DISPUTE- A consumer who seeks to dispute the accuracy of information shall provide a dispute notice directly to such person at the address specified by the person for such notices that--

(i) identifies the specific information that is being disputed;

(ii) explains the basis for the dispute; and

(iii) includes all supporting documentation required by the furnisher to substantiate the basis of the dispute.

(E) DUTY OF PERSON AFTER RECEIVING NOTICE OF DISPUTE- After receiving a notice of dispute from a consumer pursuant to subparagraph (D), the person that provided the information in dispute to a consumer reporting agency shall--

(i) conduct an investigation with respect to the disputed information;

(ii) review all relevant information provided by the consumer with the notice;

(iii) complete such person's investigation of the dispute and report the results of the investigation to the consumer before the expiration of the period under section 611(a)(1) within which a consumer reporting agency would be required to complete its action if the consumer had elected to dispute the information under that section; and

(iv) if the investigation finds that the information reported was inaccurate, promptly notify each consumer reporting agency to which the person furnished the inaccurate information of that determination and provide to the agency any correction to that information that is necessary to make the information provided by the person accurate.

(F) FRIVOLOUS OR IRRELEVANT DISPUTE-

(i) IN GENERAL- This paragraph shall not apply if the person receiving a notice of a dispute from a consumer reasonably determines that the dispute is frivolous or irrelevant, including--

(I) by reason of the failure of a consumer to provide sufficient

information to investigate the disputed information; or

(II) the submission by a consumer of a dispute that is substantially the same as a dispute previously submitted by or for the consumer, either directly to the person or through a consumer reporting agency under subsection (b), with respect to which the person has already performed the person's duties under this paragraph or subsection (b), as applicable.

(ii) NOTICE OF DETERMINATION - Upon making any determination under clause (i) that a dispute is frivolous or irrelevant, the person shall notify the consumer of such determination not later than 5 business days after making such determination, by mail or, if authorized by the consumer for that purpose, by any other means available to the person.

(iii) CONTENTS OF NOTICE - A notice under clause (ii) shall include--

(I) the reasons for the determination under clause (i); and

(II) identification of any information required to investigate the disputed information, which may consist of a standardized form describing the general nature of such information.

and

§ 623. (b) Duties of furnishers of information upon notice of dispute.

(1) In general. After receiving notice pursuant to section 611(a)(2) [§ 1681i] of a dispute with regard to the completeness or accuracy of any information provided by a person to a consumer reporting agency, the person shall

(A) conduct an investigation with respect to the disputed information;

(B) review all relevant information provided by the consumer reporting agency pursuant to section 611(a)(2) [§ 1681i];

(C) report the results of the investigation to the consumer reporting agency;

(D) if the investigation finds that the information is incomplete or inaccurate, report those results to all other consumer reporting agencies to which the person furnished the information and that compile and maintain files on consumers on a nationwide basis; and

(E) if an item of information disputed by a consumer is found to be inaccurate or incomplete or cannot be verified after any reinvestigation under paragraph (1), for purposes of reporting to a consumer reporting agency only, as appropriate, based on the results of the reinvestigation promptly --

(i) modify that item of information;

(ii) delete that item of information; or

(iii) permanently block the reporting of that item of information.

In Layman's Terms

Professional Driver Reveals Rapid Credit Repair System

Now that your head is spinning with all that law, here is what is really means.

Basically, you can dispute information placed on your credit report by an original creditor in the same way as you would with a credit bureau. An original creditor must do the following.

Conduct an investigation of the dispute.

Review all information provided by the consumer relating to the dispute.

Respond within 30 days to the investigation.

If the information is inaccurate, they must notify the credit bureaus of the mistake and tell the credit bureau to correct it.

However, the creditor can also determine the dispute is frivolous just like a credit bureau can. Some reasons as to why a dispute may be frivolous.

You just disputed the same thing without changing the reason for the dispute.

You haven't provided enough information for the creditor to conduct an investigation. At the minimum, you need to identify the account by account number and provide a reason why you are disputing.

If the creditor does determine the dispute is frivolous, they must notify you in writing by any other means available to the person within 5 days.

If the Creditor Fails to Comply with the Law

If the original creditor fails to comply with your dispute, they are in violation of the FCRA, but you can't sue them unless you have disputed with the Credit Bureaus first.

Disputing with the credit bureau first is not something you can shortcut or forget. In order to place the liability of reporting accurately squarely on the shoulders of the creditor, you must have disputed the listing with the credit bureaus. This means you have either online, via the telephone or in writing, disputed a listing with the credit bureaus and then WAITED FOR THE RESULTS OF THE INVESTIGATION.

Here is the law which enforces the fact that you must dispute with the credit bureau first:

§ 623. (c) LIMITATION ON LIABILITY- Except as provided in section 621(c)(1)(B), sections 616 and 617 do not apply to any violation of--

(1) subsection (a) of this section, including any regulations issued thereunder;

(2) subsection (e) of this section, except that nothing in this paragraph shall limit, expand, or otherwise affect liability under section 616 or 617, as applicable, for violations of subsection (b) of this section;

Sections 616 and 617 of the FCRA talk about how much the fines are for violations of the FCRA (the willful and negligent non compliance), typically $1,000.

What the above section of the FCRA § 623(c) means is that if you dispute with the original creditors first, without having disputing through the credit bureaus, and they refuse to answer you, or provide you with

proof, yes, they are in violation of the FCRA, but you as a private citizen cannot take them to court and sue them; only your state authorities (like your state attorney general) or federal authorities (like the FTC) can sue them.

However, if you have disputed the information with the credit bureaus first, they are supposed to have talked to the original creditor, even though we know that doesn't happen, and the original creditor is supposed to have at that time conducted an investigation, under FCRA § 623(b), under which you, as a private citizen can sue them. When you go to the original creditor under FCRA § 623(a)(8), you are just merely asking for the OC's proof that they must have provided to the credit bureaus during the OC's thorough investigation. If they have no proof of negative information, but the credit bureau says that the results of the investigation show the negative information is accurate, then you have the OC on an actionable, sue-able (by you) offense.

Once again, YOU MUST DISPUTE WITH THE CREDIT BUREAUS FIRST - Have we said this often enough??

Steps to Dispute with Original Creditor
What is the exact procedure when you want to dispute things with the original creditor?
The Steps:
Dispute the listing with the credit bureau.
Wait for the results of the investigation.
If the listing is deleted or modified per your desires, you're done!
If the information furnisher does not get back to you within 30 days:
You need to send a letter to the company's legal department informing them they are in violation of the FCRA and you intend to sue if they do not remove the listing.
If they do not remove the listing, you will have to sue if you want to get it off.
If the information furnisher says the results of the investigation is verified, then:
Call up the credit card company and ask them what kind of documentation they have to prove the negative mark. Many times they will have nothing.

Professional Driver Reveals Rapid Credit Repair System

Letter to the Original Debtor

Your Name
Address
City, State
Zip
SSN: 000-00-0000 | DOB: 1/1/1970

Bank of America
P.O. Box 4568
Dallas, TX 75013

Dear Legal Department:

Re: Acct #XXXXXXXX

This letter is in regards to a phone call I placed to your company regarding the account listed above on <Insert Date>.

I called to inquire about this account that is listed on my Credit Reports. I spoke to **<Insert Customer Service Representative named>** and her employee number is **<Insert #>,** as provided by her. She informed me that your company does not have any information on this account that it was all sent to a collection agency. How did you investigate this account without any documentation? I contacted the collection agency your rep told me about and they could not validate the debt. This collection agency subsequently removed all information regarding this account from my credit reports. If this incorrect information is not removed from my credit reports, I will file suit against your company.

First Name

Last Name

Email

Phone

Zip Code

IN WITNESS WHEREOF, the said party has signed and sealed these presents the day and year first above written. Signed, sealed and

Professional Driver Reveals Rapid Credit Repair System

If you need help go to my website:

UrbanCreditSecrets.com or email me at

UrbanCreditRepairSolutions@gmail.com   Jason Kirkwood

delivered in the presence of:
{PRINT   YOUR   NAME   HERE}
_____ Signature

STATE OF
COUNTY OF
I HEREBY CERTIFY that on this day before me, an officer duly qualified to take acknowledgments, personally appeared
{   YOUR   NAME   HERE   },   who   has   produced
_____ as identification
and who executed the foregoing instrument and he/she acknowledged before me that he/she executed the same.

WITNESS my hand and official seal in the County and State aforesaid this _____ day of _____2016.

_____ Notary Public

Printed Name
My commission expires:

Professional Driver Reveals Rapid Credit Repair System

www.ingramcontent.com/pod-product-compliance
Lightning Source LLC
Chambersburg PA
CBHW071223220526
45468CB00002B/709